Off to the

Child

Mouse

Bear

Gardener

Clown

Child: Hello, Mouse.
I'm on my way.
I'm on my way
to the shop.

Mouse: Hello, Child.
What will you buy?
What will you buy
at the shop?

2

3

Child: Frozen peas.

Mouse: Frozen peas?
Why don't you
buy some cheese?
I'd rather have cheese
than frozen peas,
if I went to the shop.

5

Child: Hello, Bear.
I'm on my way.
I'm on my way
to the shop.

Bear: Hello, Child.
What will you buy?
What will you buy
at the shop?

7

 Child: A piece of cheese.

 Bear: A piece of cheese?
Get a honeycomb
made by bees.
I'd buy a honeycomb
with my money,
if I went to the shop.

9

Child: Hello, Gardener.

I'm on my way.

I'm on my way

to the shop.

Gardener: Hello, Child.

What will you buy?

What will you buy

at the shop?

11

 Child: A honeycomb.

 Gardener: A honeycomb?
Why don't you buy
a garden gnome?
I'd get my home
a garden gnome,
if I went to the shop.

12

13

 Child: Hello, Clown.
I'm on my way.
I'm on my way
to the shop.

 Clown: Hello, Child.
What will you buy?
What will you buy
at the shop?

15

Child: A garden gnome.

Clown: A garden gnome?
A garden gnome
is nice at home.
I'd get a stick
to do a trick,
if I went to the shop.

17

Child: I'm coming home.
I'm coming home.
I'm coming home
from the shop.

All: What did you buy?
What did you buy?
What did you buy
at the shop?

19

Child: I meant to try
to choose and buy
a funny stick
to do a trick,
a gnome for the home,
a honeycomb,
a piece of cheese,
or some frozen peas.

21

 Child: But, sad to say
the door was shut.
I got to the shop
at half past eight,
but that was
half an hour too late.

22

23

All: But you saved
your money,
so isn't that great?
Let's have a party
to celebrate!